Love Songs by Sara Teasdale

Sara Trevor Teasdale was born on August 8, 1884 in St Louis, Missouri. A woman of poor health it was only at 14 that she was well enough to begin school. Her education finished in 1903 at Hosmer Hall and her first poetry publication was in 1907 with her second book in 1911.

She was courted by various men among them Vachel Lindsay, a great poet but one who thought he could not provide a suitable standard of living for Sara so she married Ernst Filsinger in 1914. Sara's third poetry collection, 'Rivers to the Sea', was published in 1915 and was a best seller, being reprinted many times.

A year later, in 1916 the married couple moved to New York City.

In 1917 she released the poetry collection 'Love Songs' and the following year it won three awards: the Columbia University Poetry Society prize, the 1918 Pulitzer Prize for poetry and the annual prize of the Poetry Society of America.

By 1929 Sara was deeply unhappy and lonely so she moved out of state for three months in order to gain a divorce. She did not wish to inform Filsinger, and only at the insistence of her lawyers as the divorce was going through did she. Filsinger was naturally shocked and surprised to now discover the truth.

After her divorce Sara remained in New York City and resumed her friendship with Vachel Lindsay, who was by this time married with children.

1931 Vachel Lindsay committed suicide. Two year on 29th January 1933 Sara Teasdale, at the age of 48, committed suicide by overdosing on sleeping pills. She is buried in the Bellefontaine Cemetery in St. Louis.

Index of Contents

The Song for Colin
Four Winds
Debt
Faults
Buried Love
The Fountain
I Shall Not Care
After Parting
A Prayer
Spring Night
May Wind
Tides
After Love
New Love and Old
The Kiss
Swans
The River
November
Spring Rain
The Ghost
Summer Night, Riverside
Jewels

II

Interlude: Songs out of Sorrow
I - Spirit's House
II - Mastery
III - Lessons
IV - Wisdom
V - In a Burying Ground
VI - Wood Song
VII - Refuge

III

The Flight
Dew
To-night
Ebb Tide
I Would Live in Your Love
Because
The Tree of Song
The Giver
April Song
The Wanderer
The Years
Enough
Come
Joy
Riches
Dusk in War Time

To E.

I have remembered beauty in the night,
Against black silences I waked to see
A shower of sunlight over Italy
And green Ravello dreaming on her height;
I have remembered music in the dark,
The clean swift brightness of a fugue of Bach's,
And running water singing on the rocks
When once in English woods I heard a lark.

But all remembered beauty is no more
Than a vague prelude to the thought of you—
You are the rarest soul I ever knew,
Lover of beauty, knightliest and best;
My thoughts seek you as waves that seek the shore,
And when I think of you, I am at rest.

I

Barter

Life has loveliness to sell,
All beautiful and splendid things,
Blue waves whitened on a cliff,
Soaring fire that sways and sings,
And children's faces looking up
Holding wonder like a cup.

Life has loveliness to sell,

Music like a curve of gold,
Scent of pine trees in the rain,
Eyes that love you, arms that hold,
And for your spirit's still delight,
Holy thoughts that star the night.

Spend all you have for loveliness,
Buy it and never count the cost;
For one white singing hour of peace
Count many a year of strife well lost,
And for a breath of ecstasy
Give all you have been, or could be.

Twilight

Dreamily over the roofs
The cold spring rain is falling;
Out in the lonely tree
A bird is calling, calling.

Slowly over the earth
The wings of night are falling;
My heart like the bird in the tree
Is calling, calling, calling.

Night Song at Amalfi

I asked the heaven of stars
What I should give my love—
It answered me with silence,
Silence above.

I asked the darkened sea
Down where the fishers go—
It answered me with silence,
Silence below.

Oh, I could give him weeping,
Or I could give him song—
But how can I give silence,
My whole life long?

The Look

Strephon kissed me in the spring,
Robin in the fall,
But Colin only looked at me
And never kissed at all.

Strephon's kiss was lost in jest,
Robin's lost in play,
But the kiss in Colin's eyes
Haunts me night and day.

A Winter Night

My window-pane is starred with frost,
The world is bitter cold to-night,
The moon is cruel, and the wind
Is like a two-edged sword to smite.

God pity all the homeless ones,
The beggars pacing to and fro,
God pity all the poor to-night
Who walk the lamp-lit streets of snow.

My room is like a bit of June,
Warm and close-curtained fold on fold,
But somewhere, like a homeless child,
My heart is crying in the cold.

A Cry

Oh, there are eyes that he can see,
And hands to make his hands rejoice,
But to my lover I must be
Only a voice.

Oh, there are breasts to bear his head,
And lips whereon his lips can lie,
But I must be till I am dead
Only a cry.

Gifts

I gave my first love laughter,
I gave my second tears,
I gave my third love silence
Through all the years.

My first love gave me singing,
My second eyes to see,
But oh, it was my third love
Who gave my soul to me.

But Not to Me

The April night is still and sweet
With flowers on every tree;
Peace comes to them on quiet feet,
But not to me.

My peace is hidden in his breast
Where I shall never be;
Love comes to-night to all the rest,
But not to me.

Song at Capri

When beauty grows too great to bear
How shall I ease me of its ache,
For beauty more than bitterness
Makes the heart break.

Now while I watch the dreaming sea
With isles like flowers against her breast,
Only one voice in all the world
Could give me rest.

Child, Child

Child, child, love while you can
The voice and the eyes and the soul of a man;
Never fear though it break your heart—
Out of the wound new joy will start;
Only love proudly and gladly and well,

Though love be heaven or love be hell.

Child, child, love while you may,
For life is short as a happy day;
Never fear the thing you feel—
Only by love is life made real;
Love, for the deadly sins are seven,
Only through love will you enter heaven.

Love Me

Brown-thrush singing all day long
In the leaves above me,
Take my love this April song,
"Love me, love me, love me!"

When he harkens what you say,
Bid him, lest he miss me,
Leave his work or leave his play,
And kiss me, kiss me, kiss me!

Pierrot

Pierrot stands in the garden
Beneath a waning moon,
And on his lute he fashions
A fragile silver tune.

Pierrot plays in the garden,
He thinks he plays for me,
But I am quite forgotten
Under the cherry tree.

Pierrot plays in the garden,
And all the roses know
That Pierrot loves his music,—
But I love Pierrot.

Wild Asters

In the spring I asked the daisies
If his words were true,

And the clever, clear-eyed daisies
Always knew.

Now the fields are brown and barren,
Bitter autumn blows,
And of all the stupid asters
Not one knows.

The Song for Colin

I sang a song at dusking time
Beneath the evening star,
And Terence left his latest rhyme
To answer from afar.

Pierrot laid down his lute to weep,
And sighed, "She sings for me."
But Colin slept a careless sleep
Beneath an apple tree.

Four Winds

"Four winds blowing through the sky,
You have seen poor maidens die,
Tell me then what I shall do
That my lover may be true."
Said the wind from out the south,
"Lay no kiss upon his mouth,"
And the wind from out the west,
"Wound the heart within his breast,"
And the wind from out the east,
"Send him empty from the feast,"
And the wind from out the north,
"In the tempest thrust him forth;
When thou art more cruel than he,
Then will Love be kind to thee."

Debt

What do I owe to you
Who loved me deep and long?
You never gave my spirit wings

Or gave my heart a song.

But oh, to him I loved,
Who loved me not at all,
I owe the open gate
That led through heaven's wall.

Faults

They came to tell your faults to me,
They named them over one by one;
I laughed aloud when they were done,
I knew them all so well before,—
Oh, they were blind, too blind to see
Your faults had made me love you more.

Buried Love

I have come to bury Love
Beneath a tree,
In the forest tall and black
Where none can see.

I shall put no flowers at his head,
Nor stone at his feet,
For the mouth I loved so much
Was bittersweet.

I shall go no more to his grave,
For the woods are cold.
I shall gather as much of joy
As my hands can hold.

I shall stay all day in the sun
Where the wide winds blow,—
But oh, I shall cry at night
When none will know.

The Fountain

All through the deep blue night
The fountain sang alone;

It sang to the drowsy heart
Of the satyr carved in stone.

The fountain sang and sang,
But the satyr never stirred—
Only the great white moon
In the empty heaven heard.

The fountain sang and sang
While on the marble rim
The milk-white peacocks slept,
And their dreams were strange and dim.

Bright dew was on the grass,
And on the ilex, dew,
The dreamy milk-white birds
Were all a-glisten, too.

The fountain sang and sang
The things one cannot tell;
The dreaming peacocks stirred
And the gleaming dew-drops fell.

I Shall Not Care

When I am dead and over me bright April
Shakes out her rain-drenched hair,
Though you should lean above me broken-hearted,
I shall not care.

I shall have peace, as leafy trees are peaceful
When rain bends down the bough,
And I shall be more silent and cold-hearted
Than you are now.

After Parting

Oh, I have sown my love so wide
That he will find it everywhere;
It will awake him in the night,
It will enfold him in the air.

I set my shadow in his sight
And I have winged it with desire,

That it may be a cloud by day,
And in the night a shaft of fire.

A Prayer

Until I lose my soul and lie
Blind to the beauty of the earth,
Deaf though shouting wind goes by,
Dumb in a storm of mirth;

Until my heart is quenched at length
And I have left the land of men,
Oh, let me love with all my strength
Careless if I am loved again.

Spring Night

The park is filled with night and fog,
The veils are drawn about the world,
The drowsy lights along the paths
Are dim and pearled.

Gold and gleaming the empty streets,
Gold and gleaming the misty lake,
The mirrored lights like sunken swords,
Glimmer and shake.

Oh, is it not enough to be
Here with this beauty over me?
My throat should ache with praise, and I
Should kneel in joy beneath the sky.
O, beauty, are you not enough?
Why am I crying after love,
With youth, a singing voice, and eyes
To take earth's wonder with surprise?

Why have I put off my pride,
Why am I unsatisfied,—
I, for whom the pensive night
Binds her cloudy hair with light,—
I, for whom all beauty burns
Like incense in a million urns?
O beauty, are you not enough?
Why am I crying after love?

May Wind

I said, "I have shut my heart
As one shuts an open door,
That Love may starve therein
And trouble me no more."

But over the roofs there came
The wet new wind of May,
And a tune blew up from the curb
Where the street-pianos play.

My room was white with the sun
And Love cried out in me,
"I am strong, I will break your heart
Unless you set me free."

Tides

Love in my heart was a fresh tide flowing
Where the starlike sea gulls soar;
The sun was keen and the foam was blowing
High on the rocky shore.

But now in the dusk the tide is turning,
Lower the sea gulls soar,
And the waves that rose in resistless yearning
Are broken forevermore.

After Love

There is no magic any more,
We meet as other people do,
You work no miracle for me
Nor I for you.

You were the wind and I the sea—
There is no splendor any more,
I have grown listless as the pool
Beside the shore.

But though the pool is safe from storm
And from the tide has found surcease,
It grows more bitter than the sea,
For all its peace.

New Love and Old

In my heart the old love
Struggled with the new;
It was ghostly waking
All night through.

Dear things, kind things,
That my old love said,
Ranged themselves reproachfully
Round my bed.

But I could not heed them,
For I seemed to see
The eyes of my new love
Fixed on me.

Old love, old love,
How can I be true?
Shall I be faithless to myself
Or to you?

The Kiss

I hoped that he would love me,
And he has kissed my mouth,
But I am like a stricken bird
That cannot reach the south.

For though I know he loves me,
To-night my heart is sad;
His kiss was not so wonderful
As all the dreams I had.

Swans

Night is over the park, and a few brave stars

Look on the lights that link it with chains of gold,
The lake bears up their reflection in broken bars
That seem too heavy for tremulous water to hold.

We watch the swans that sleep in a shadowy place,
And now and again one wakes and uplifts its head;
How still you are—your gaze is on my face—
We watch the swans and never a word is said.

The River

I came from the sunny valleys
And sought for the open sea,
For I thought in its gray expanses
My peace would come to me.

I came at last to the ocean
And found it wild and black,
And I cried to the windless valleys,
"Be kind and take me back!"

But the thirsty tide ran inland,
And the salt waves drank of me,
And I who was fresh as the rainfall
Am bitter as the sea.

November

The world is tired, the year is old,
The fading leaves are glad to die,
The wind goes shivering with cold
Where the brown reeds are dry.

Our love is dying like the grass,
And we who kissed grow coldly kind,
Half glad to see our old love pass
Like leaves along the wind.

Spring Rain

I thought I had forgotten,
But it all came back again

To-night with the first spring thunder
In a rush of rain.

I remembered a darkened doorway
Where we stood while the storm swept by,
Thunder gripping the earth
And lightning scrawled on the sky.

The passing motor busses swayed,
For the street was a river of rain,
Lashed into little golden waves
In the lamp light's stain.

With the wild spring rain and thunder
My heart was wild and gay;
Your eyes said more to me that night
Than your lips would ever say. . . .

I thought I had forgotten,
But it all came back again
To-night with the first spring thunder
In a rush of rain.

The Ghost

I went back to the clanging city,
I went back where my old loves stayed,
But my heart was full of my new love's glory,
My eyes were laughing and unafraid.

I met one who had loved me madly
And told his love for all to hear—
But we talked of a thousand things together,
The past was buried too deep to fear.

I met the other, whose love was given
With never a kiss and scarcely a word—
Oh, it was then the terror took me
Of words unuttered that breathed and stirred.

Oh, love that lives its life with laughter
Or love that lives its life with tears
Can die—but love that is never spoken
Goes like a ghost through the winding years. . . .

I went back to the clanging city,

I went back where my old loves stayed,
My heart was full of my new love's glory,—
But my eyes were suddenly afraid.

Summer Night, Riverside

In the wild, soft summer darkness
How many and many a night we two together
Sat in the park and watched the Hudson
Wearing her lights like golden spangles
Glinting on black satin.
The rail along the curving pathway
Was low in a happy place to let us cross,
And down the hill a tree that dripped with bloom
Sheltered us,
While your kisses and the flowers,
Falling, falling,
Tangled my hair. . . .

The frail white stars moved slowly over the sky.

And now, far off
In the fragrant darkness
The tree is tremulous again with bloom,
For June comes back.

To-night what girl
Dreamily before her mirror shakes from her hair
This year's blossoms, clinging in its coils?

Jewels

If I should see your eyes again,
I know how far their look would go—
Back to a morning in the park
With sapphire shadows on the snow.

Or back to oak trees in the spring
When you unloosed my hair and kissed
The head that lay against your knees
In the leaf shadow's amethyst.

And still another shining place
We would remember—how the dun

Wild mountain held us on its crest
One diamond morning white with sun.

But I will turn my eyes from you
As women turn to put away
The jewels they have worn at night
And cannot wear in sober day.

II

Interlude: Songs Out of Sorrow

I

Spirit's House

From naked stones of agony
I will build a house for me;
As a mason all alone
I will raise it, stone by stone,
And every stone where I have bled
Will show a sign of dusky red.
I have not gone the way in vain,
For I have good of all my pain;
My spirit's quiet house will be
Built of naked stones I trod
On roads where I lost sight of God.

II

Mastery

I would not have a god come in
To shield me suddenly from sin,
And set my house of life to rights;
Nor angels with bright burning wings
Ordering my earthly thoughts and things;
Rather my own frail guttering lights
Wind blown and nearly beaten out;
Rather the terror of the nights
And long, sick groping after doubt;
Rather be lost than let my soul
Slip vaguely from my own control—
Of my own spirit let me be

In sole though feeble mastery.

III

Lessons

Unless I learn to ask no help
From any other soul but mine,
To seek no strength in waving reeds
Nor shade beneath a straggling pine;
Unless I learn to look at Grief
Unshrinking from her tear-blind eyes,
And take from Pleasure fearlessly
Whatever gifts will make me wise—
Unless I learn these things on earth,
Why was I ever given birth?

IV

Wisdom

When I have ceased to break my wings
Against the faultiness of things,
And learned that compromises wait
Behind each hardly opened gate,
When I can look Life in the eyes,
Grown calm and very coldly wise,
Life will have given me the Truth,
And taken in exchange—my youth.

V

In a Burying Ground

This is the spot where I will lie
When life has had enough of me,
These are the grasses that will blow
Above me like a living sea.

These gay old lilies will not shrink
To draw their life from death of mine,
And I will give my body's fire

To make blue flowers on this vine.

"O Soul," I said, "have you no tears?
Was not the body dear to you?"
I heard my soul say carelessly,
"The myrtle flowers will grow more blue."

VI

Wood Song

I heard a wood thrush in the dusk
Twirl three notes and make a star—
My heart that walked with bitterness
Came back from very far.

Three shining notes were all he had,
And yet they made a starry call—
I caught life back against my breast
And kissed it, scars and all.

VII

Refuge

From my spirit's gray defeat,
From my pulse's flagging beat,
From my hopes that turned to sand
Sifting through my close-clenched hand,
From my own fault's slavery,
If I can sing, I still am free.

For with my singing I can make
A refuge for my spirit's sake,
A house of shining words, to be
My fragile immortality.

III

The Flight

Look back with longing eyes and know that I will follow,
Lift me up in your love as a light wind lifts a swallow,
Let our flight be far in sun or blowing rain—
But what if I heard my first love calling me again?

Hold me on your heart as the brave sea holds the foam,
Take me far away to the hills that hide your home;
Peace shall thatch the roof and love shall latch the door—
But what if I heard my first love calling me once more?

Dew

As dew leaves the cobweb lightly
Threaded with stars,
Scattering jewels on the fence
And the pasture bars;
As dawn leaves the dry grass bright
And the tangled weeds
Bearing a rainbow gem
On each of their seeds;
So has your love, my lover,
Fresh as the dawn,
Made me a shining road
To travel on,
Set every common sight
Of tree or stone
Delicately alight
For me alone.

To-night

The moon is a curving flower of gold,
The sky is still and blue;
The moon was made for the sky to hold,
And I for you.

The moon is a flower without a stem,
The sky is luminous;
Eternity was made for them,
To-night for us.

Ebb Tide

When the long day goes by
And I do not see your face,
The old wild, restless sorrow
Steals from its hiding place.

My day is barren and broken,
Bereft of light and song,
A sea beach bleak and windy
That moans the whole day long.

To the empty beach at ebb tide,
Bare with its rocks and scars,
Come back like the sea with singing,
And light of a million stars.

I Would Live in Your Love

I would live in your love as the sea-grasses live in the sea,
Borne up by each wave as it passes, drawn down by each wave that recedes;
I would empty my soul of the dreams that have gathered in me,
I would beat with your heart as it beats, I would follow your soul
as it leads.

Because

Oh, because you never tried
To bow my will or break my pride,
And nothing of the cave-man made
You want to keep me half afraid,
Nor ever with a conquering air
You thought to draw me unaware—
Take me, for I love you more
Than I ever loved before.

And since the body's maidenhood
Alone were neither rare nor good
Unless with it I gave to you
A spirit still untrammeled, too,
Take my dreams and take my mind
That were masterless as wind;
And "Master!" I shall say to you
Since you never asked me to.

The Tree of Song

I sang my songs for the rest,
For you I am still;
The tree of my song is bare
On its shining hill.

For you came like a lordly wind,
And the leaves were whirled
Far as forgotten things
Past the rim of the world.

The tree of my song stands bare
Against the blue—
I gave my songs to the rest,
Myself to you.

The Giver

You bound strong sandals on my feet,
You gave me bread and wine,
And sent me under sun and stars,
For all the world was mine.

Oh, take the sandals off my feet,
You know not what you do;
For all my world is in your arms,
My sun and stars are you.

April Song

Willow, in your April gown
Delicate and gleaming,
Do you mind in years gone by
All my dreaming?

Spring was like a call to me
That I could not answer,
I was chained to loneliness,
I, the dancer.

Willow, twinkling in the sun,

Still your leaves and hear me,
I can answer spring at last,
Love is near me!

The Wanderer

I saw the sunset-colored sands,
The Nile like flowing fire between,
Where Rameses stares forth serene,
And Ammon's heavy temple stands.

I saw the rocks where long ago,
Above the sea that cries and breaks,
Swift Perseus with Medusa's snakes
Set free the maiden white like snow.

And many skies have covered me,
And many winds have blown me forth,
And I have loved the green, bright north,
And I have loved the cold, sweet sea.

But what to me are north and south,
And what the lure of many lands,
Since you have leaned to catch my hands
And lay a kiss upon my mouth.

The Years

To-night I close my eyes and see
A strange procession passing me—
The years before I saw your face
Go by me with a wistful grace;
They pass, the sensitive, shy years,
As one who strives to dance, half blind with tears.

The years went by and never knew
That each one brought me nearer you;
Their path was narrow and apart
And yet it led me to your heart—
Oh, sensitive, shy years, oh, lonely years,
That strove to sing with voices drowned in tears.

Enough

It is enough for me by day
To walk the same bright earth with him;
Enough that over us by night
The same great roof of stars is dim.

I do not hope to bind the wind
Or set a fetter on the sea—
It is enough to feel his love
Blow by like music over me.

Come

Come, when the pale moon like a petal
Floats in the pearly dusk of spring,
Come with arms outstretched to take me,
Come with lips pursed up to cling.

Come, for life is a frail moth flying,
Caught in the web of the years that pass,
And soon we two, so warm and eager,
Will be as the gray stones in the grass.

Joy

I am wild, I will sing to the trees,
I will sing to the stars in the sky,
I love, I am loved, he is mine,
Now at last I can die!

I am sandaled with wind and with flame,
I have heart-fire and singing to give,
I can tread on the grass or the stars,
Now at last I can live!

Riches

I have no riches but my thoughts,
Yet these are wealth enough for me;
My thoughts of you are golden coins
Stamped in the mint of memory;

And I must spend them all in song,
For thoughts, as well as gold, must be
Left on the hither side of death
To gain their immortality.

Dusk in War Time

A half-hour more and you will lean
To gather me close in the old sweet way—
But oh, to the woman over the sea
Who will come at the close of day?

A half-hour more and I will hear
The key in the latch and the strong, quick tread—
But oh, the woman over the sea
Waiting at dusk for one who is dead!

Peace

Peace flows into me
As the tide to the pool by the shore;
It is mine forevermore,
It will not ebb like the sea.

I am the pool of blue
That worships the vivid sky;
My hopes were heaven-high,
They are all fulfilled in you.

I am the pool of gold
When sunset burns and dies—
You are my deepening skies;
Give me your stars to hold.

Moods

I am the still rain falling,
Too tired for singing mirth—
Oh, be the green fields calling,
Oh, be for me the earth!

I am the brown bird pining
To leave the nest and fly—
Oh, be the fresh cloud shining,
Oh, be for me the sky!

Houses of Dreams

You took my empty dreams
And filled them every one
With tenderness and nobleness,
April and the sun.

The old empty dreams
Where my thoughts would throng
Are far too full of happiness
To even hold a song.

Oh, the empty dreams were dim
And the empty dreams were wide,
They were sweet and shadowy houses
Where my thoughts could hide.

But you took my dreams away
And you made them all come true—
My thoughts have no place now to play,
And nothing now to do.

Lights

When we come home at night and close the door,
Standing together in the shadowy room,
Safe in our own love and the gentle gloom,
Glad of familiar wall and chair and floor,

Glad to leave far below the clanging city;
Looking far downward to the glaring street
Gaudy with light, yet tired with many feet,
In both of us wells up a wordless pity;

Men have tried hard to put away the dark;
A million lighted windows brilliantly
Inlay with squares of gold the winter night,
But to us standing here there comes the stark
Sense of the lives behind each yellow light,

And not one wholly joyous, proud, or free.

"I Am Not Yours"

I am not yours, not lost in you,
Not lost, although I long to be
Lost as a candle lit at noon,
Lost as a snowflake in the sea.

You love me, and I find you still
A spirit beautiful and bright,
Yet I am I, who long to be
Lost as a light is lost in light.

Oh plunge me deep in love—put out
My senses, leave me deaf and blind,
Swept by the tempest of your love,
A taper in a rushing wind.

Doubt

My soul lives in my body's house,
And you have both the house and her—
But sometimes she is less your own
Than a wild, gay adventurer;
A restless and an eager wraith,
How can I tell what she will do—
Oh, I am sure of my body's faith,
But what if my soul broke faith with you?

The Wind

A wind is blowing over my soul,
I hear it cry the whole night through—
Is there no peace for me on earth
Except with you?

Alas, the wind has made me wise,
Over my naked soul it blew,—
There is no peace for me on earth
Even with you.

Morning

I went out on an April morning
All alone, for my heart was high,
I was a child of the shining meadow,
I was a sister of the sky.

There in the windy flood of morning
Longing lifted its weight from me,
Lost as a sob in the midst of cheering,
Swept as a sea-bird out to sea.

Other Men

When I talk with other men
I always think of you—
Your words are keener than their words,
And they are gentler, too.

When I look at other men,
I wish your face were there,
With its gray eyes and dark skin
And tossed black hair.

When I think of other men,
Dreaming alone by day,
The thought of you like a strong wind
Blows the dreams away.

Embers

I said, "My youth is gone
Like a fire beaten out by the rain,
That will never sway and sing
Or play with the wind again."

I said, "It is no great sorrow
That quenched my youth in me,
But only little sorrows
Beating ceaselessly."

I thought my youth was gone,

But you returned—
Like a flame at the call of the wind
It leaped and burned;

Threw off its ashen cloak,
And gowned anew
Gave itself like a bride
Once more to you.

Message

I heard a cry in the night,
A thousand miles it came,
Sharp as a flash of light,
My name, my name!

It was your voice I heard,
You waked and loved me so—
I send you back this word,
I know, I know!

The Lamp

If I can bear your love like a lamp before me,
When I go down the long steep Road of Darkness,
I shall not fear the everlasting shadows,
Nor cry in terror.

If I can find out God, then I shall find Him,
If none can find Him, then I shall sleep soundly,
Knowing how well on earth your love sufficed me,
A lamp in darkness.

IV

A November Night

There! See the line of lights,
A chain of stars down either side the street—
Why can't you lift the chain and give it to me,
A necklace for my throat? I'd twist it round
And you could play with it. You smile at me

As though I were a little dreamy child
Behind whose eyes the fairies live. . . . And see,
The people on the street look up at us
All envious. We are a king and queen,
Our royal carriage is a motor bus,
We watch our subjects with a haughty joy. . . .
How still you are! Have you been hard at work
And are you tired to-night? It is so long
Since I have seen you—four whole days, I think.
My heart is crowded full of foolish thoughts
Like early flowers in an April meadow,
And I must give them to you, all of them,
Before they fade. The people I have met,
The play I saw, the trivial, shifting things
That loom too big or shrink too little, shadows
That hurry, gesturing along a wall,
Haunting or gay—and yet they all grow real
And take their proper size here in my heart
When you have seen them. . . . There's the Plaza now,
A lake of light! To-night it almost seems
That all the lights are gathered in your eyes,
Drawn somehow toward you. See the open park
Lying below us with a million lamps
Scattered in wise disorder like the stars.
We look down on them as God must look down
On constellations floating under Him
Tangled in clouds. . . . Come, then, and let us walk
Since we have reached the park. It is our garden,
All black and blossomless this winter night,
But we bring April with us, you and I;
We set the whole world on the trail of spring.
I think that every path we ever took
Has marked our footprints in mysterious fire,
Delicate gold that only fairies see.
When they wake up at dawn in hollow tree-trunks
And come out on the drowsy park, they look
Along the empty paths and say, "Oh, here
They went, and here, and here, and here! Come, see,
Here is their bench, take hands and let us dance
About it in a windy ring and make
A circle round it only they can cross
When they come back again!" . . . Look at the lake—
Do you remember how we watched the swans
That night in late October while they slept?
Swans must have stately dreams, I think. But now
The lake bears only thin reflected lights
That shake a little. How I long to take
One from the cold black water—new-made gold

To give you in your hand! And see, and see,
There is a star, deep in the lake, a star!
Oh, dimmer than a pearl—if you stoop down
Your hand could almost reach it up to me. . . .

There was a new frail yellow moon to-night—
I wish you could have had it for a cup
With stars like dew to fill it to the brim. . . .

How cold it is! Even the lights are cold;
They have put shawls of fog around them, see!
What if the air should grow so dimly white
That we would lose our way along the paths
Made new by walls of moving mist receding
The more we follow. . . . What a silver night!
That was our bench the time you said to me
The long new poem—but how different now,
How eerie with the curtain of the fog
Making it strange to all the friendly trees!
There is no wind, and yet great curving scrolls
Carve themselves, ever changing, in the mist.
Walk on a little, let me stand here watching
To see you, too, grown strange to me and far. . . .
I used to wonder how the park would be
If one night we could have it all alone—
No lovers with close arm-encircled waists
To whisper and break in upon our dreams.
And now we have it! Every wish comes true!
We are alone now in a fleecy world;
Even the stars have gone. We two alone!

www.ingramcontent.com/pod-product-compliance
Lightning Source LLC
Chambersburg PA
CBHW060047050426
42448CB00012B/3140